THRILL RIDES

VALERIE BODDEN

FERRIS WHEELS

THRILL RIDES

VALERIE BODDEN

Creative Education

Published by Creative Education P.O. Box 227, Mankato, Minnesota 56002 Creative Education is an imprint of The Creative Company www.thecreativecompany.us
Design and art direction by Rita Marshall Production by The Design Lab Printed by Corporate Graphics in the United States of America Photographs by Alamy (MIXA), Corbis
(Plainpicture), Dreamstime (Michael Klenetsky, Vladislav Romensky, David Wigner), iStockphoto (A-Digit, Yong Hian Lim, Maya Kovacheva Photography), Shutterstock (Alita
Bobrov, Jordache, George Pappas, Pitcha T, Slasha, Hans Van Camp, Visuelldesign, Xjbxjhxm123) Copyright © 2012 Creative Education International copyright reserved in
all countries. No part of this book may be reproduced in any form without written permission from the publisher. Library of Congress Cataloging-in-Publication Data Bodden,
Valerie. Ferris wheels / by Valerie Bodden. p. cm. — (Thrill rides) Summary: A colorful survey of Ferris wheels, including their cars and other features, descriptions of the ride
experience, and a brief history. Famous Ferris wheels such as the London Eye are spotlighted. Includes bibliographical references and index. ISBN 978-1-60818-113-1 1.
Ferris wheels—Juvenile literature. I. Title. GV1860.F45B63 2012 791.06'8—dc22 2010049381 CPSIA: 030111 PO1450 First Edition 9 8 7 6 5 4 3 2 1

FERRIS WHEELS

TABLE OF CONTENTS

UP, UP, AND AROUND.

THE Ferris wheel turns. Its riders are lifted toward the sky. They feel like they are flying!

A Ferris wheel is a ride made of a big wheel that spins. Cars for riders are attached to the rim, or edge, of the wheel. Ferris wheels can be found at **amusement parks**, fairs, and carnivals.

A Ferris wheel is held up by towers. **Spokes** lead from the middle of the wheel to its rim. They make the wheel strong. Some Ferris wheel cars are small and open. Others have a roof and glass sides. These big cars can hold many people.

Carnival Ferris wheels

BEFORE riding most Ferris wheels, you have to be measured to make sure you are tall enough for the ride. The wheel stops with a car at the bottom to let you on. On most Ferris wheels, a lap bar is fastened over you. Then the wheel begins to turn! Most Ferris wheel rides last 3 to 10 minutes.

AS a Ferris wheel turns, its cars sway. The ride is gentle, but it is exciting to be so high! Some Ferris wheels glow with colorful lights.

SOME kinds of Ferris wheels are wilder. A double Ferris wheel has two wheels on a large beam that turns. On sliding Ferris wheels, some of the cars slide from the rim of the wheel to its center.

A double Ferris wheel

IN the 1600s, people in **Europe** (*YOO-rup*) built small, wooden "pleasure wheels." They were turned by people. Later, **engines** were added.

 1893, George Washington Gale Ferris built a huge **steel** wheel in Chicago, Illinois. It could hold 2,160 people! After that, pleasure wheels were called Ferris wheels.

Singapore Flyer

TODAY, the world's tallest Ferris wheel is the Singapore Flyer in Singapore. It is 541 feet (165 m) tall! An even taller Ferris wheel is being built in China.

THE Big O in Japan is the biggest Ferris wheel without spokes. A roller coaster passes through its center! Every Ferris wheel is different—and every Ferris wheel can be a thrilling ride!

Big O

London Eye

ONE FAMOUS FERRIS WHEEL

Name: London Eye

Location: London, England

Year Opened: 2000

Height: 443 feet (135 m)

The London Eye was built to celebrate the year 2000. This Ferris wheel's cars have a roof and glass sides. Each car can hold 25 people. Until 2006, the London Eye was the tallest Ferris wheel in the world. From the top, riders can see things as far as 25 miles (40 km) away!

GLOSSARY

amusement parks—outdoor areas where people pay to go on rides, play games, or see shows

engines—machines that use energy to make things, such as cars or rides, move

Europe—one of Earth's continents, or large areas of land, with many countries such as France, Spain, and Germany

Singapore—an island country in Southeast Asia, south of China

spokes—rods that reach from the middle, or hub, of a wheel to its rim to help support the wheel

steel—a very hard, strong metal that is usually gray in color

READ MORE

Alter, Judy. *Amusement Parks: Roller Coasters, Ferris Wheels, and Cotton Candy.* New York: Watts, 1997.

Crews, Donald. *Night at the Fair.* New York: Greenwillow Books, 1998.

WEB SITES

Ferris Wheels of the World
http://www.travel-images.com/ferris-wheels.html
See pictures of some of the most amazing Ferris wheels in the world.

Preschool Coloring Book: Amusement Parks
http://www.preschoolcoloringbook.com/color/cpamuse.shtml
Color pictures of all your favorite amusement park rides and activities.

INDEX